Coming
From the
HEART
of a
LEADER

By Portia Daniels

ISBN-13: 978-1523420094

ISBN-10: 152342009X

Dedication

This book is dedicated first to God, then to every leader who is always striving for excellence in all that they do.

Contents

Acknowledgements

I would like to thank everyone who has supported me, provided continued encouragement and accountability throughout my journey in writing and publishing this book. Just to name a few, I want to personally thank my parents for always believing in me, Chris and Dr. Joy Allen for always seeing the best in me and challenging me to bring it out, and Shannon DeVaughn for being the best friend that anyone could ever ask for. To all those that were not specifically mentioned, know that I appreciate you and I thank you! I'm so grateful to be surrounded by such awesome and beautiful people.

Introduction

Many aspiring leaders and even experienced leaders believe that in order to lead effectively you must be in a position of authority. In fact, many books are focused on leading from this perspective. I will admit that I have struggled with this belief for many years until I came to know a better way and it catapulted me to where I am today. I am driven by impacting lives and that has inspired me to write this book in hopes of doing just that. In this book, I focus on teaching leaders that you can indeed lead effectively even if you don't have a position because it is a part of who you are. Leadership is influence through service and when this is understood any person can do it no matter what their role may be. I will share my personal experiences and the things that I have learned over the past five years working in the pharmaceutical industry and will provide practical knowledge that any leader can use.

In this book, I share thirteen lessons on leadership that will provide you with principles and strategies for self-improvement and greater influence. Each lesson falls under one of three categories which include what leadership really is, the principles to be applied before you lead and the principles to be applied when you lead. Lesson one will be addressed in the first category that discusses what leadership really is. It sets the foundation for all the other lessons that will follow. Lessons two through eight will be addressed in the second category that discusses the principles that need to be applied before you lead. These are all lessons that need to be addressed within yourself or they will be hindrances to your influence. Lessons nine through thirteen will be addressed in the third category that discusses the principles that need to be applied when you are leading. They really focus on how to work with those around you. At the end of each lesson, a personal challenge will be issued that will encourage you to examine where you are and an assignment is given that will aid you in improving in that area. If you desire to be an excellent leader, then you will enjoy this book.

Lesson #1

Leadership is not a position but who you are

Have you ever had a professor in college or a presentation given for a quarterly meeting at work that you didn't understand? When I think about the issue of leadership and position, I am reminded of two different experiences that I had years ago with two of my previous college professors who had very different teaching styles. One professor taught physics and the other taught neuroscience. Both were very challenging courses at that time but I didn't have the same learning experience with each. The first professor that taught physics was not only knowledgeable but he also had a great teaching ability. Everyone loved him and wanted to be in his class because he had a way of taking the complicated concepts in physics and breaking them down into simple terms that anyone could comprehend the lessons. His instruction was very engaging and he used examples that students could relate to. The second professor that taught neuroscience was very knowledgeable as well but he taught by just reading PowerPoint presentations. Honestly, I felt that it was a little boring and I couldn't say that I had a great learning experience in class. I wouldn't leave feeling connected and with a good understanding of the material.

When I pondered on these two examples, it occurred to me that just because someone holds a position of a professor and has a great depth of knowledge does not mean that they are an effective teacher. It is the same with leadership. Just because someone holds a position in leadership does not mean they are an effective leader nor does it mean that a position can make you a leader. It is not about having a position to lord over people and manipulate them in such a way that you get them to do any and everything that pleases you. Leadership is about influencing others through serving them in such a way that adds value to them. You can certainly do this whether you are the head honcho or an individual contributor. It is a leader's role to empower people to be the best that they can be and not the best that you want them to be. They do not look to make followers and people who will be dependent upon them but they give them the tools that they need to flourish and they create an environment to realize growth. Leaders not only focus on what they can teach people but also how they can pull out the best in others. For the longest time, I felt like I needed a position to validate me as a leader and that only then would I be able to lead and make an impact on the lives of those around me. Then, I realized that this was certainly not the case and it became my goal to impact the lives of those around me in the workplace, my family and my community. This thing extends way beyond a position at work.

Now that we know that leadership is not about a position, there are two key things to keep in mind that will help us to exercise leadership skills in any capacity within or without a position.

- **Leadership is a part of who you are.** It is a part of your identity. Along my journey, I had to realize that you have to know who you are because your actions will follow what you believe about yourself. If you do not believe that you are a leader, then you simply will not operate as one. Even if you do it for a little while, you won't be consistent when challenges and opposition come if you are not convinced yourself. When it's a part of who you are, you can't get away from it. Even at a young age, I remember taking up for others who couldn't or wouldn't take up for themselves. I remember saying to myself that I wanted to make a difference in the world but I had no idea what that would mean for me. No one taught me to think that way or to do certain things, it came natural to me in my childhood but I didn't know it back then. Even after realizing this as an adult, I struggled for so long to believe that a position or a title did not define me as a person. Going back to the validation issue, I would work so hard to obtain a leadership role, not so I could help others, but because in a sense I still felt like I needed it to validate me and give me permission to add values to others. I'm so much more than that and so are you. When you're just being who you are, people will look to as an encouragement and you may not even know it.

- **Leadership ability is a gift.** Much like any other gift it is to be discovered, cultivated and perfected. I've often heard discussions about whether leaders are born or made. I must say that I do not subscribe to either ideology. I believe that those who are truly leaders have a desire and a heart to lead. That's not something you can just teach or force on people. In addition to having a heart to lead, I believe that your leadership abilities along with your character have to be developed so that what you do can be excellent. It's a package deal and it should be taken seriously. It does not matter what position you may hold, if you don't have the package deal then you will not be good at leading. Many people are good at managing people and processes but not leading.

Personal Challenge for Lesson #1

Questions to Ask Yourself: Do you believe that you are a leader? Even if you don't receive immediate praise and acknowledgment for it, would you still do it? If so, what are some things that you can start doing to serve someone else?

Assignment: Decide that you will be intentional about leading others. Every day, make it your goal to add value to at least one person. Some examples of how this could be done includes sending an encouraging note to a colleague to show your appreciation and support, volunteering to teach others something new that you've learned that would be useful to them, doing a random act of kindness or challenging someone else to see their potential by affirming them in their strengths. When you commit to this, you may be surprised to see how much of a difference it makes.

Bottom Line: Don't lead to get a position but do it because it is a part of who you are and then you'll be more impactful and more prepared for when you do step into the leadership role that you aspire to be in.

Coming From the Heart of a Leader

Lesson #2

Face Your Insecurities and Embrace Your Uniqueness

If we'll be honest, we all have areas where we are insecure and it is okay. We just have to be willing to recognize them and address them in the proper way so that we can overcome them. Insecurities come when we experience an unfavorable situation or when we come into contact with someone who speaks against the truth of who we are. Some of it could also be due to mistakes we've made in the past that we haven't gotten over. When these types of things happen, it makes us feel that we are not good enough or it makes us doubt whether we have what it takes to get the job done. It hinders us from leading with confidence and with the best of who we are. I remember times in my life when I would be in the midst of a group of people and it would be easy for me to fade into the background and act as if I wasn't there because of my insecurities that I hadn't really dealt with. One of the main reasons why it was easy for me to fade into the background is because I still felt like everyone else had something great to offer except for me. It seemed like people would easily look over me because I wasn't the type that easily became the center of attention. When I had something to say, I would belittle it even before people had a chance to hear me out. I would say things like "it's just my opinion" or "you don't have to listen if you don't want to". I would literally talk myself out of being confident. If that wasn't enough, I would try to justify everything that I said or be overly apologetic when all I needed to do was simply say what I had to say and leave it at that.

Not dealing with your insecurities, especially as a leader, can be very detrimental to your influence. Here are some common effects.

- **Everything becomes about you.** If your motive for leadership is self-centered then you already set yourself up for failure because once you decide that you want to be a leader your life no longer remains just about you but it turns into how you can use your life to help someone else. Many so often turn leadership into a tool for them to be served and be put on a pedestal. Their focus is primarily on proving themselves and making people respect them. Our goal should be to show people how great they are and have the potential to be and not how great we are.

- **Intimidation.** When you are intimidated by other people, you intentionally or even secretly desire to hold them back because in your mind they become a threat to you. Even if someone has something that they can contribute to you, you won't receive it and return you hinder your own growth. When you are working with others you will either compete with them or shrink back all together instead of collaborating with them.

- **Manipulation and Control.** This is not the right kind of influence that we want to have. This may be done intentionally and unintentionally. People should do things with and for you because they want to and not because you pressured them to do it. People will naturally want to help you when they see that you genuinely care about them. There should be a mutual benefit.

- **Cloudy vision.** Insecurity will cloud your vision of yourself, your life and others. You will begin to see yourself and what you have to offer to be worthless or unimportant. You will you see your life as sucky and something to just get through rather than an opportunity to grow and make a change. You will treat others the way that you wouldn't want to be treated.

In order to properly address and combat our insecurities there are some tools that we should grab a hold of.

- **Face it.** You can't overcome what you're not willing to acknowledge. Examine yourself. That's the first step. Oftentimes, we don't like to deal with it because it's uncomfortable but it's essential that we do. If not, it will continue to follow us and influence our thoughts and actions.

- **Confidence is a choice.** You have to choose to walk in confidence. You do have control over this thing. When those negative thoughts that you have rehearsed time and time again, come to you, you can choose whether you will allow them to dictate your actions and how you carry yourself or if you will be guided by confidence. The more you invest and concentrate on being your best the more confident you will become.

- **Embrace your uniqueness.** It's okay to be different. Get to know you and the beauty that is within you. Celebrate and appreciate yourself. Then you will be able to do the same for others. What you have to offer is needed and special. For instance, I am very organized and analytical but I would find myself surrounded by others that weren't the best organized and didn't care about dissecting every little detail of everything. For quite some time, I thought I needed to be more like them rather than seeing how our differences can bring a healthy balance. I had to learn that I couldn't focus so much on how great other people were that I could no longer see my own greatness.

- **Don't compare yourself with others.** When you compare yourself with other people, you actually limit yourself and make them the standard which is ridiculous when you really think about it. We should use others as an encouragement but not the standard. If you really knew your potential, if you really knew what you had going for you then you would realize that you no longer have to look at other people and think that you are less than or that you don't somehow measure up. If you see that someone has what you feel you lack, if you can change it, simply learn what you can from them and change it. If you can't change it, accept the fact that it's okay and just share what others need from you.

Personal Challenge for Lesson #2

Questions to Ask Yourself: What are the areas where you are insecure? How can it or has it impacted your leadership? What can you begin to do to overcome in those areas?

Assignment: Think about one or two areas where you are insecure and how those viewpoints came to be in your life. Decide that you will work to overcome in those areas by doing something different. This may mean stopping the cycle of settling for less than what's best for you, finding someone to confide in who will be there to build you up or separating yourself from those negative people and situations that have caused you to feel insecure. Then, think about 5 great qualities that are unique to who you are and spend more time focusing on those qualities than you do on the ones you don't like.

Bottom Line: Don't cover up or avoid your insecurities because they will follow you wherever you go if not dealt with. Make peace with yourself and don't hide your greatness.

Lesson #3

Be Committed to Constant Growth

During my 11th grade year in high school, I took up algebra and I absolutely loved it. It was one of my favorite subjects and one of my strengths. I aced all of my quizzes, exams and homework assignments with ease. Truthfully speaking, I never paid attention to the teacher because all of my learning took place when I read the textbook and completed the homework assignments. All of my classmates would be so impressed with my test scores and would wonder how I did so well but it wasn't a big deal to me because it was in my strength zone and it was never challenging at all. However, it was a completely different story when I was encouraged to take up Pre-Calculus. I thought that the same amount of effort that I had been giving before would work then but I was so wrong. I quickly discovered that it wasn't going to be as easy as I thought it was and it would actually take some work. You would think that I would step up my efforts in order to excel in this class as I did in Algebra but I didn't. I continued to do average work and I got an average grade at the end. When I reflected on this time in my life, I learned a valuable lesson about how important it is to be committed to constant growth.

Commit to the growth process! It's a gradual thing and it's never ending. If you desire to go to the next level, if you desire to be great, if you desire to offer the best to others then you must be willing to go through a growth process. You have to be willing to invest in yourself so that you can offer your best and become the leader that you would want to follow. You can only get out what you put in. In order to grow you have to be willing to do things that you've never done before. You have to be willing to stretch yourself and be uncomfortable. If the truth were told, as humans, we like to be comfortable and we like stability. Even working in the pharmaceutical industry over the years, there were always changes in processes and systems and you just had to go with the flow. I always wondered why there were always new changes right after everyone was just getting used to the previous wave of change. I soon realized that in order for a company to remain on the cutting edge they had to continue evolving and expanding. It's the same attitude that we have to have about ourselves. If you're not willing to change so that you can grow you will remain stagnant.

When we think about the growth process there are few things to be considered.

- **Increase your knowledge but don't get stuck there.** More knowledge does not equal growth and maturity. I am a knowledge sponge. I love to research and learn new things and I can get content there. I may even get content in just reflecting on how what I've learned applies to my life but at some point I must put what I've learned into action. It's when we've applied the things that we've learned that will then open the door for growth to show up. Knowledge can also give us a false estimation of ourselves. Too much knowledge can make us feel like we are better than others because we know what they do not know so we end up teaching them what they should be doing while we don't apply the same principles ourselves.

- **Value Preparation.** Preparation never feels good but the reward comes when it's time for you to show up to do the job and deliver. For instance, when I am preparing a presentation or a training session, I put a lot of work into studying the material and making sure that the information is organized in a way that makes sense. Sometimes, I get nervous and I question whether I'll be able to fulfill the audience's expectations but when it's time for me to deliver, everything works out and I'm glad that I continued to press to that point. We all want to just show up great on day one but it doesn't work that way. Preparation isn't easy but it's worth it in the end.

- **Don't depend on your gifts and talents.** When you are naturally gifted or talented to do something well it can be very tempting to just wing it because you can get by with it. It's not about doing the bare minimum to get by but doing your work in excellence and being a person with good character. Even in your strength zones, you have to challenge yourself. Capitalize on those areas so that you can perfect your craft. Don't focus so much on your weak zones unless you are able to change them. For instance, your character qualities such as integrity, faithfulness, and kindness are examples of things that could be changed if you are weak in those areas. Some areas where you may not be able to change may include math skills, artistic abilities or dominant extroverted and introverted tendencies. You may be able to adjust in these areas just to get the job done but the likelihood of you doing a complete one eighty are slim to none because it's not a part of your makeup.

- **Be open to continued constructive criticism.** We will never arrive. It is a scary thing to think that you have arrived because then you are saying that you have no more room to grow. I don't know how many stories I've heard of people reaching a certain place in life or in obtaining a certain position and they feel like I've put in my time and I've done this thing for so long that there's nothing more than I can learn and there's nothing that anyone can teach me. We're all a work in progress. I know for sure that I wouldn't be the person I am today if I didn't have people in my life that told me the truth about what I needed to improve on even if it wasn't something that I wanted to hear but I had to be humble enough to listen. Humility does not mean that you are unsure of yourself and should take everything that someone says to you but it means that you don't have an overestimated opinion of yourself and you're open to being taught by others no matter who they are. If you are settled with the applause of others, you'll always be good but never be great. Both praise and constructive criticism have their place.

- **See challenging situations and people as growth opportunities.** We've all experienced difficult situations or people at some point in our lives. Sometimes we're so focused on how a person is treating us and how hard things may be instead of looking at it as an opportunity for growth and maturity. We become victims of our circumstances when we allow them to make us worse off instead of better. We don't have control over people but we can control ourselves. It starts with taking the ownership of how we respond. There was a time in my life where I dealt with a difficult manager. She didn't really provide the support that I needed and didn't make me feel as though she wanted me to succeed. Though I didn't feel like I was being treated fairly, that still did not give me an excuse to be disrespectful to her and slack of in my work. I had to allow the situation to challenge me to be a person of integrity even when it's hard to do. No matter what we go through there is a lesson to be learned. It could be that we learn something new about ourselves and where we need improvement or it could be lessons on what not to do in the future.

- **Learn the art of resilience.** This is important when it comes to bouncing back from a major life change or career change that wasn't expected. We have to embrace change. It's inevitable. Since we cannot avoid it, we should ride the waves and stick it out instead of resisting it. Another reason that resilience is important is because we will make mistakes and we have to be accustomed to learning from those mistakes and not beating ourselves up about it and allowing other people to beat us up about it. Believe it or not, failure and mistakes are a part of the growth process too.

Personal Challenge for Lesson #3

Questions to Ask Yourself: Where do you struggle in your growth process? How have you hindered yourself from growing? What can you do about it?

Assignment: Think about the top three areas in the growth process where you need improvement. Decide on one action that you can do to move forward in each of those areas. For instance, if one of your areas is that you have a lot of knowledge in a particular area that you haven't applied, an action item could be to commit to looking for ways to apply it immediately or making it up in your mind that you will no longer seek out more knowledge without the intention of applying what you've learned.

Bottom Line: Leaders should be growing constantly. Embrace the process because it will make you better.

Lesson #4

Change Your Environment, Change You

Have you ever taken a moment to admire all the beautiful flowers that grow in the spring and summer seasons? We'll look at them and admire their beauty. We'll even use them for interior and exterior decorations in our offices and homes. However, they didn't start out as something beautiful. They started as seeds. They started out as something plain, nothing extravagant. In order for the seeds to grow and blossom into the flowers that we can now enjoy, they had to be in an environment that was conducive to their growth. Now, I'm not a florist by any means but I do understand that there are different components that play a role in their environment such as sunlight, soil, temperature and water. If one of those components were missing they wouldn't be able to experience change. It is the same with us and the environment that we keep in our lives. Our environment plays a huge role in who we are today and who we will become tomorrow. It is a fallacy to believe that we can change and get to the next place where we desire to be without changing our environment.

There are four components that make up our environment. As a leader, you will need to make sure that you have the right settings in each in order to become a better influencer.

- **Mindset.** Everything starts in our minds. Our mindset is influenced by our personality, values, beliefs, experiences, relationships and the things that we listen to. How we view life and different situations is very important. We have to discover and get rid of our mindset barriers that will hinder us from moving forward. One of the biggest and most common mindset barriers, that even I have to constantly fight against, is stinking thinking. If we don't think that we'll overcome then we won't. If we think that everyone is against us, without good reason to feel this way, then that's how we'll treat everyone who we cross paths with. We have to train our minds to have a winning attitude no matter what the obstacles are that we may be facing. If we don't have a winning attitude then we are automatically giving ourselves permission to give up on our goals and become victims of our circumstances.

- **Speaking.** We have to be mindful of what is coming out of our mouths. What you say not only affects you but it also affects other people. Our mouths can get us into trouble or it can save us from trouble. It can build up a person or tear them down. Speak well of others and speak well of yourself as much as possible. Say things that are affirming and uplifting. Communicate a grateful and winning attitude. Don't complain about everything. When there are hard deadlines to meet at work and everyone is stressed, a leader should be the one to motivate others and get them to see the good rather than jumping on the compliant bandwagon. That doesn't mean that you don't live in reality and acknowledge it when something is wrong but it's in the way you say it and the motive behind it. If we acknowledge something that's negative, we should find a way to solve it or put a positive spin on it. Negativity and complaining is intoxicating.

- **Information and Resources.** We have to be mindful of the information and resources that we are surrounded by. We all live our lives according to what we know. We won't do better if we don't at least know better and see better. That's why it's important to go to conferences, join professional associations, take up new classes, read new books, read new articles, etc. All these things will enhance us as individuals and give us more of a reservoir to pull from so that we can in turn enhance other people. We can't give to others what we don't have. We have to see ourselves as a gift to others. If you saw yourself in this way, what would your gift look like?

Would it look old and used up or would it look fresh and vibrant? Would others be happy or disappointed to receive such a gift? Keep in mind the type of gift that you want to be to others.

- **People.** We should surround ourselves with three types of people, those who are where we desire to be and can challenge and push us, those who are our colleagues and peers who keep us accountable and we encourage each other, and those who we can teach and help get to where we are. We are typically surrounded by our peers and that's fine but we also have to be mindful to surround ourselves with people in the other two categories and they may even overlap. Here are more details about the people in each of those areas.

    1) **People who are where we desire to be-** we need people who will challenge and push us to go to the next level and who have the knowhow to get us there. Oftentimes, these are people who are able to see the potential in us that we may not see in ourselves. Life's challenges can cause us to suppress the greatness that's on the inside of us and we need someone to help pull it out. These could also be people who challenge us to think bigger and pass what we have allowed to be limitations in our lives. They

don't have to necessarily be leading you in the same area. I am a firm believer in having multiple mentors or advisors. No one person can teach you everything. You could also put people in this category that you may not know personally but you watch them from a distance and learn how they do things.

2) **Our colleagues and peers-** these are people who tend to be our friends who are in the same boat with you in that you are all trying to get to the same place. You encourage and sharpen one another. You grow together and teach each other new things. You bounce ideas off of each other and use each other to practice your leadership skills on.

3) **Those who desire to be where we are-** these are people who we can teach and pour into, who are either coming into who they are and want to get to where you are or people who are weak in areas where you are stronger. You don't have to be in a leadership position to mentor or teach someone. People can tell if you are a resource that they can go to by the way you act and how you carry yourself. You don't have to necessarily announce it. Just do it. For

instance, in a work environment, be the person who is knowledgeable and is always looking to share that knowledge with others.

Personal Challenge for Lesson #4

Questions to Ask Yourself: What does your environment look like? What do you need to change about it?

Assignment: Pick one area in your life where your environment needs to change. As you think about this area, consider the four components of an environment that were mentioned in this lesson. Then, think about what your current settings are in those components and identify what needs to improve. For instance, leadership as whole may be an area of your life where your environment needs to change. Then, when you look at the four components, you may see that you need to change the people that you surround yourself with or the resources that are available to you.

Bottom Line: We are influenced and shaped by our environment. Create the environment that you need to be the person that you desire to be.

Lesson #5

Confidence and Presentation Matters

A dear friend of mine that I hadn't seen in years came to visit from out of town to attend a wedding for a mutual friend of ours. When I learned of the news that she would be in town, I was so ecstatic and couldn't wait for us to catch up on life during the short period of time that she would be in the area. Once we finally got a chance to meet up, I learned that she recently had a career change and became a recruiter for a staffing agency and how she had been growing from different experiences. At some point, we got into a discussion about how your appearance not only affects your mood but it also affects how others view you. She began to tell me about how different her experiences were with the leadership and with her coworkers when she decided to dress based on where she wanted to go and who she wanted to be. She started to dress like a business professional and just by the way she dressed she distinguished herself from others and people automatically thought that her role was more important than it actually was. As a result of this, she gained respect with everyone. She was amazed by how differently she was being treated and how she was getting a lot of positive feedback from those who weren't providing it in the past by doing something as little as changing the way she looked. As a leader, confidence and presentation is huge. If you are not confident in yourself, your abilities and in what you know, then people will not be confident in you either. In the same token, if you are not presenting yourself a certain way then people will not take you seriously. Whether it's intentional or not, people will treat you based on the way you carry yourself.

Presentation is more than just about the way you look but it's about carrying yourself well. There are a few factors that I have learned that play a major part in the issue of confidence and presentation.

- **Portraying confidence.** You have to learn how to portray confidence even if you don't feel it in the moment. I'm not necessarily talking about faking it until you make it. However, I am stressing the importance of getting over yourself, pressing past how you feel, and disciplining yourself to choose confidence. Even if you doubt yourself at times, that can't come across especially when you are leading. It doesn't matter how much you know, if you are unsure of yourself and you come across that way people will doubt your competence, integrity and ability to follow through. You really wouldn't be able to fault them for it either. After all, what motivation have you given them to be reassured in following you? I've also noticed that even if you are not completely competent and may even be completely wrong about something people will still be willing to follow you because your confidence is attractive to them. That's how serious it is. Think about it this way. When you go on a job interview, you typically don't act like you don't have what it takes but you put your best foot forward because you are trying to get the interviewer's buy in. It's not just about portraying confidence but you also have to build your confidence and that comes through competence, investing in yourself, preparation and following through when you make commitments to get things done.

- **Appearance.** Your appearance does matter, especially, if you are trying to build a reputation for yourself. One of my mentors once said, don't dress for where you are but dress for where you want to go. People who are dressing for where they want to go don't show up for work in a corporate setting with jeans and a t-shirt. There's a certain level of professionalism to be upheld. The way you dress affects your mindset about yourself as well as the mindset that others have when they think about you. There have been times when I have literally avoided speaking to certain people because I didn't like what I had on. I was having an off day and I was ashamed of the way I looked. On the days that I looked great and I knew I looked great, I had more confidence to speak to people and engage in conversation when I wouldn't have otherwise. It's not just about the clothes you have on but it also includes the way you wear your hair, wearing decent shoes, making sure your facial hair is shaved and nails groomed. For women, it may even include putting on a little makeup. Doing something so small can make a hug difference and they are things that people will actually notice. Before you walk out the door in the morning, make sure it's a look that you are proud of and are comfortable with. Aim to look your best and then you will act as such.

- **The way you speak.** In the words of one my mentors "it's not what you say but how you say it". Everything you say should be thoughtful, intelligent, and with purpose and conviction. The way you speak includes things such as being professional, articulate and controlled. You have to take control of your emotions and keep your face even in difficult situations. Sometimes we think that we're good if we don't say anything but in fact our facial expressions will say what we're not saying. Don't spaz out in front of everyone just because you are frustrated and stressed out. Be mindful of how your words influence others. The way we speak can cause people to trust or doubt our abilities. Our mouths are a tool that can build people up or tear them down. Our words can bring peace to a situation or they can add more fuel to the fire in a hostile situation. We can be so focused on ourselves that we completely forget how much of an impact what we say has on whether people will want to work with us and how people will take what we have mentioned to make life decisions. When I worked in project management, I took a public speaking course that the company had offered for professional development. It was an all-day training and as a part of the training we of course had to practice presenting on different topics. For one of the topics, we were requested to speak on something that we were passionate about. I ended up choosing to present on healthy relationships, what they look like, how to develop them and so on. I spoke from my experiences of having a great friend in my life. Unbeknownst to me, one of the project directors took the information that I shared and gave it to her daughter who was dealing with a difficult relationship in order to assist her in the dilemma that she was currently facing. When she shared that with me, not only was I encouraged but it also reminded me of the fact that what you say really does influence people whether or not you are aware of it.

- **How you are perceived by others.** The way we come across to people does matter. Sometimes we need to take inventory of ourselves and how we are coming across to others. Sometimes we really don't realize how other people view us until we actually stop and take the time to really think about it. One way to identify how people perceive you is by thinking about the type of feedback that you are getting. If people are coming to you with the same issues and you are common denominator, then more than likely that is an area that you need to work on. In those cases, I wouldn't just take it with a grain of salt. There's something to be said when the same message is being communicated to us. I mentioned before that I am an introvert at heart so sometimes it takes effort for me to interact with people, especially, if it is for an extended amount of time and without previously having developed a relationship a with them. Due to this, I often come across to others as antisocial, distant or as if I'm better than them. However, I didn't realize this until more than one person began to express in some way or another that they didn't feel comfortable talking to me. I also got feedback from those whom I trust and who know my heart and even they would tell me that they could see how I was being perceived that way even though it wasn't me. This perception wasn't necessarily because I wasn't friendly or nice to people. It was because I wasn't mindful to take a little extra effort to connect with those around me so that they wouldn't take me the wrong way. This also meant that I had to be willing to step outside of my comfort zone. Now, there may be some things that you may not be able to change but if it's within your control, adapting without completely losing yourself is worth considering if it may affect your ability to work with others.

Personal Challenge for Lesson #5

Questions to Ask Yourself: What do you want your presentation to represent? What do you want others to think about when they see you? Do your desires and views actually match how people really see you?

Assignment: Make a note of the qualities that you want to be known for. It could be that you want people to know you as caring, excellent, professional, knowledgeable and authentic. Once you have identified these qualities, ask three people that you trust how they would describe you and if they would agree that you are consistent with your desired qualities. Try to diversify the list of people that you receive feedback from. If there are inconsistencies then decide if and how you need to adjust. By doing this exercise, you may even find new things about yourself that you hadn't paid attention to before.

Bottom Line: Carry yourself well and be mindful of your presentation. It will certainly impact people's perceptions of you and ultimately how they treat you.

Lesson #6

The Connection between Decisiveness and Assertiveness

I don't know anyone who's great at decision making yet doesn't know how to be assertive. The two feed one another. One of the hardest things to do is work with someone who can never make a decision about anything or doesn't know how to verbalize what's really on their mind. I've struggled with both and things began to change for me when I saw the effects of it and I got sick of it being a hindrance to my influence. Now, I will outline how the two are related and provide a few lessons that I had to implement in order to see the growth that I desired.

Decisiveness means that you are able to make up your mind about what it is that you are going to do, what you are going to stand for and the willingness to commit to the choice that you have made. When you are indecisive, people start to automatically doubt you because the message that you are sending to others is instability. Here are some ways that we can be become more decisive.

- **Make a decision to be a decisive person.** Habits aren't developed overnight nor will they be broken overnight. When you have developed a pattern of being indecisive about things, you have to be intentional about making a change so that you can catch yourself in those moments that you may tend to want to revert back. This is also true even if you don't consider this to be a great weakness for yourself but know there's still room for improvement. You have to find a way to hold yourself accountable. This may even require that you ask others to hold you accountable. You have to have a mindset that says it's not enough to try, either you do or you don't.

- **Find out what it is that you really want.** Sometimes it's hard for us to make a decision because we simply do not know what we want or we're not honest about what we really want. It boils down to what's really important to you and prioritizing those things. You have to be clear on this because no one can tell you what it is. Figure out what you want to accomplish, how you want to be treated, what you want to represent, what your core values are etc.

- **Pick a side.** I'm sure we've all been in team meetings where a decision was pending on a particular issue so a consensus had to be taken. You always have three groups of people, those who agree with the decision on the issue, those who disagree and those who can never pick a side. Those who can never make up their mind are typically not useful in that moment especially if they can't even explain why that is their stance. No matter which group you may find yourself in, you have to be willing and able to communicate the reasoning behind it.

- **Learn the process of making good decisions.** There are some decisions that you'll need to be able to make instantly under pressure, some that are not that serious and won't require a lot of time and others that are very important such as life changing matters that may require some time for you to decide. You don't have to take all day to decide on something that may not be that serious like where to go to eat for dinner with your friends or what to wear to work. If you are married with a family and you get a job offer that's in another state, then that would require more time. No matter the issue that you are facing, there are some things that you can consider in order to make a good decision. Get informed. Ask questions if you need to. Weigh the pros and cons. Take some time to really think about it. Contemplate long enough until you can come to a decision that you are comfortable with. Don't be so concerned about making a bad decision that you don't make one at all. Even if you do make a mistake, it's not the end of the world and it can be used as a learning opportunity.

Assertiveness means that you are able to communicate to others, with assurance and without apologies, that which you have made a decision about. It could be your decision about the standards you have set for yourself or your unique perspective on things. When you fail to be assertive, people will automatically not take you seriously and feel like they can treat you any kind of way. Here are some ways that you can become more assertive.

- **Speak up for yourself.** It is no one else's responsibility to speak up for you except you. You are not a bad person because you choose to take up for yourself. You set the standard for how you want people to treat you because if you don't someone else will. You are a person with real thoughts, feelings and opinions that should be heard too. You don't just have to accept crap from others just because they're giving it out and you don't have to justify every decision that you make if it's your business. Don't let people walk all over you in the name of peace. Sure there are times when it's more beneficial to keep silent because not every action requires a response. For some things you may have to hit the ignore button. There also comes a point where we have to deal with it verbally or else nothing will change. Many times we think of the negative consequences that may come with taking up for ourselves but we may not consider the positive consequences of it. On one end it's beneficial to you, in that it boosts your confidence and allows you to move forward and not hold unnecessary grudges. On the other end it's beneficial to others, in that you may bring something to their attention that they need to work on which they hadn't considered before, it may encourage others who are looking at you to be the same way and people will learn to respect you for it. As a clinical coordinator, I had a coworker who was from Germany so she was very honest and direct about what was on her mind. If she disagreed with a process or if she felt that timelines to complete a given task were unrealistic she would undoubtedly say something. Though she had issues with coming off a little harsh at times, I appreciated her because I never had to doubt where she stood.

- **Stand your ground.** Even if it's not popular. You have to be willing to go against the grain if that's what the situation will require. Standing your ground is beyond standing up for yourself but also standing up for a cause that you believe in and what you believe in your heart is the right thing to do. You have to be able to defend yourself and not be moved just because someone disagrees. You don't have to break when your standards and views are questioned. Don't quickly fold at the sign of opposition. You can be respectful and still disagree with someone. Having a viewpoint that is different from someone else doesn't necessarily mean that you cannot work with them. In some cases, you have to agree to disagree so that everyone can move on and the team effort not be hindered. People don't want to follow someone who changes their stance to fit the popular opinion of their current surroundings. Let your yes be yes and your no be no, no matter who the person is. The person could be a colleague or in a position of leadership but it's all in how you word it. I attended a class about powerfully presenting yourself that a professional organization was hosting and one of the things that were mentioned included the way you formulate your words and how much of a difference it makes. I agree wholeheartedly with this ideology. You can state the same thing and it be received differently because of how you presented it.

Personal Challenge for Lesson #6

Questions to Ask Yourself: In what areas of your life have you struggled to be decisive and assertive? What were the consequences? What can you do to change the negative consequences?

Assignment: Make a note of some of the primary things that you tend to be indecisive about. Consider why you tend to be indecisive in those areas and figure out what you really want. Weed out the pressures and expectations that have come from others. Then, be committed to verbalizing the decisions you've made when the opportunity presents itself. For instance, an area of indecisiveness could be how you spend your time in that you're always struggling with whether to do things for others because you're afraid that you'll disappoint them if you say no to their request. Due to this, your own goals are never met. In this case, an action could be to set a schedule that prioritizes your goals and being willing to tell others when you're not available.

Bottom Line: When you are decisive, it helps you to be more assertive. Commit to a decision and be willing to verbalize it without trying to justify it or apologize for it.

Lesson #7

Integrity is Big

When I think about the good relationships that have been developed in any area of my life versus the ones that are not so good, the difference between the two ultimately lies in an issue with having a lack of integrity and character. Those who I consider to be my friends and trusted advisors are the ones who have proven time and time again that they care enough about our relationship that they keep their commitments and they don't intentionally do things that they know would bother me. Even when they make mistakes, I don't have to doubt whether their heart is in a good place. I know that a major part of why they treat me, as well as others, the way that they do is due to their determination to be a person of integrity. I have learned to appreciate the people in those relationships because I know what it's like not to have that. The other people in the negative relationships in my life were the complete opposite. They didn't really care about my wellbeing, they would tell lies to me as well as others in an attempt to cover themselves and they always talked about what they would do but never got around to it so as a result it was difficult for me to trust anything that came out of their mouths. Though I aim to have good intentions for the most part, I too have been guilty of having shabby integrity in certain areas of my life such as not being able to complete everything on my to-do list because of overcommitting myself. In those cases, I couldn't get mad if someone had some doubts about my reliability but it was a red flag for me to change because I am committed to being a person of integrity and I wouldn't want others' perception of me to be tainted. We've all been there, either by experiencing it from the actions of others or doing it ourselves.

Here are some lessons that are advantageous and critical when it comes to being a person of integrity.

- **Your reputation does matter.** Your name should mean something to you. Not the literal meaning of your name but what it represents to others. It does indeed matter what people think, especially, if it will hinder your influence and ability to push the vision that's in your heart. No matter where you go and what you do, you should have a good name. Once it's tainted, perhaps due to a series of unwise decisions, it is very hard to gain it back. When people think about your name, they should easily be able to attest to your integrity, works of excellence, character and significance. There are certain people who have built such a good reputation for themselves that no matter what they do, no matter what their name is attached to, people will simply follow them not necessarily because they are famous but because they know that anything with their name on it is quality work and is sure to add value to their lives. That's part of the reason why it is essential to be mindful of your connections because they say something about you whether it is good or bad.

- **Don't be a hypocrite.** Practice what you preach. People will not trust the things that are coming out of your mouth if they don't see you living it out yourself. I once heard someone say "leadership is not what you do to people but with people". Don't ask others to do something that you are not willing to do yourself. Lead by example. You have to be intentional about not becoming the person that you wouldn't want to follow. Make sure you have the same qualities that you would want to see in a leader. Don't try to look the part but actually be the part. People don't need someone who's great at appearing to be something great because appearances can be deceiving but what people need more than anything is someone of substance.

- **Be truthful in all your endeavors.** You don't have to lie to people or give them false promises in order to get what you want. You don't have to put others down or scandalize their name in order to get ahead. Do what's ethical even if it's not popular or convenient. Anybody that knows me will tell you that I am a stickler for the rules. Sometimes, even to a fault. It doesn't matter what everyone else is doing, if the company policy says one thing then I will try my absolute best to live by it while in the workplace even if management isn't watching. Just because other people may take the liberty to leave work early and still charge time doesn't mean that I should do the same.

- **Be consistent.** Consistency translates to others, knowingly and unknowingly, as faithfulness and trustworthiness. Don't change who you are based on who you're around. Always be yourself. You may have to adapt a little in how you carry yourself based on your environment but you should never be a completely different person from the one that is true to who you are. Even as a leader, you should be a consistent resource for others based on your area of expertise. In the past, I was a queen of being consistently inconsistent until I got serious about being a leader. I remember being frustrated and discouraged because I would meet people who would consider me to be a resource or trusted advisor but somewhere along the way the relationship would change and they would no longer come to me for guidance and questions. When I did some self-reflection, I realized that it was because I wasn't being consistent. I wasn't a stable resource for them. Some days I would act like a leader and other days I would stay in my own little bubble and act like I didn't want to be bothered.

- **Overcome being a people pleaser.** Living to please people is a guaranteed failure. It will cause you to do things that you wouldn't ordinarily do and even things that you don't really want to do. No is not a curse word. When you get clear on your vision and the things that are most important to you, having the ability to say no can be the best thing that ever happened to you. Oftentimes, we don't want to say no to others because we are afraid of disappointing certain ones but we'll never get anywhere if we hold on to that mentality. That's how we end up over committing ourselves and getting nothing done that we initially committed to doing.

Personal Challenge for Lesson #7

Questions to Ask Yourself: What commitments have you made but didn't follow through on? What is the consistent feedback that you get from other people about yourself? Based on what you know, when people hear or see your name, what's the first thing that comes to their mind? Would they be surprised to hear that you are a person of integrity?

Assignment: Make a note of your current commitments and identify the ones that you have struggled to keep. They could also be commitments that you have coming up that you may not be able to keep. Decide how important your commitments are and whether you can realistically follow through on them. If you find that you are not able keep your word, inform the individual(s) ahead of time and possibly see if there's room for negotiation. Moving forward, put into place one action item that will help you to avoid being put in the same predicament again. For instance, an action item could be tracking your commitments on a calendar and making sure that you check it before you say yes to the next thing.

Bottom Line: Your integrity or the lack thereof will make or break your reputation with those around you. Develop such a good name for yourself that people can no longer doubt the quality of anything that you are attached to. Surround yourself with others who prioritize being a person of integrity as well.

Lesson #8

Clear Vision is Essential

For the first time in my life, I am pursuing my dreams and passions, not simply something that I am interested in or an idea that sounds good. There's a difference between being interested in something and being passionate about something. When I attended East Carolina University, I had plans on becoming a pediatrician because I enjoyed working with kids and I wanted to make good money so I majored in psychology with a minor in pre-med. It sounded like a good idea to me. However, it didn't quite work out the way I had planned it to. My last year at the university, I had the opportunity to participate in a shadowing program so I was able to work with physicians in different specialties which included pediatrics. After the program was over, I quickly realized that working with children was not my passion and something that I could stay committed to for years of study though it sounded really good on paper. At that point, I was really nervous because I had completed all of these years of studying pre-med. I was on the verge of graduating and I had no idea what I was going to do next so I decided to stick with something in the medical field. That is how I ended up in clinical research and pharmaceuticals. I figured it was along the same lines of my interests and that I would enjoy it. Mind you, I didn't really pay attention to what I might do with psychology because I was so stuck on my original plan to be in the medical field. I completely ignored what drew me into studying psychology in the first place and that was my undying desire to understand and learn people so that I could help them. I was still stuck on what sounded like a good idea.

After I started my career path in clinical research, over the years I slowly discovered that no matter what role I was in, I would find myself looking for opportunities to lead, train and mentor other people. Even if I wasn't being compensated for it, I still did it because I enjoyed it, I was good at it and it was challenging to me. You see, your passion is what drives you. It's what you live for. This time, I knew it wasn't just an interest because I couldn't get away from it. Not only did I realize that this was my niche but others saw it too. It's a beautiful thing when you discover your passion and giftings that complement it because then you will meet vision. In order to be a leader, you have to be person of vision. Leaders have vision and they know direction. A vision is something that you can see clearly and it depicts your purpose or ultimate goal. It provides guidance and gives you something that you are constantly moving towards. It keeps you focused and productive so that you are always growing and not easily distracted by other things that may come your way. Another element of vision that is very critical and often missed is that it is more than just a goal. When you really have a vision, you can't accomplish it alone. If it does not require a team of people to accomplish it, then it's really not a vision. It's supposed to be bigger than you and even a little intimidating.

Once you discover your vision, there are many factors that play into making it a reality. Here are a few to get you started.

- **Write it down.** Write your vision down and keep it before you so that you can rehearse it and remind yourself of it on a continual basis. The more you rehearse it, the more you will believe it and the more you believe it the more your actions will start to align with it. Writing it down helps you as well as others see it clearly. It also holds you accountable. When doubt creeps in, you have something in front of you that will remind you of what it is that you are doing and why you are doing it.

- **Mission.** Your mission is the how. It is a set of strategic, specific and short-term achievable goals that align with your vision. This is where the work begins. It's your roadmap to success. It doesn't matter how great of a vision you have, you will not accomplish it if you don't have the wisdom and the know how to get there. Sometimes, we don't have the wisdom and need to seek it out. Other times, we do know how to get there but we don't put the mission into action and do the work that is required.

- **Commitment.** You have to be set on your vision and completely sold out for it. You can't expect other people to follow you if you are not completely convinced of your own vision. Better yet, you won't be able to really add value to people if you do not think that your vision has any real value. You have to change the way you think about your vision. Is it a nice dream or is it a necessity? It is a necessity if it will benefit those around you and solve the problems that they have. When you see your vision as a necessity, you will be committed to it and you won't be so quick to give it up just because setbacks may come or because it may require greater sacrifice than expected.

- **Self-discipline.** There's this thing called immediate gratification. It trips so many of us up time and time again. As the saying goes "the struggle is real" but the reward for choosing to delay gratification is so worth it. It's so much greater and fulfilling in the end. Temptation will never go away so we can't put off following our vision until tomorrow. If we do we'll continue to create a cycle for ourselves and develop what I call the "I'll do better tomorrow" syndrome. In times of discouragement, we have to remember the why behind the what. Anyone who has anything worth having in life got it because they had a goal to meet and learned how to discipline themselves. They forfeited moments of instant pleasure that would have kept them from moving forward and stuck to doing what they really didn't feel like doing so that later on they could enjoy the pleasures of life after the goal was accomplished.

- **Support system.** This goes back to the point that if you really have a vision you will need a team of people in order to accomplish it. You are going to need a support system with those who are on the sidelines cheering you on and those in the trenches who are actually working with you. Envision that you're in a race and you're running with people who you have to pass the baton to so that the team can win but you also have your friends and family who are cheering you on in the stands.

- **Fight your enemies.** Anything worth having requires a fight. It's certainly not a cake walk. That same fight we have when someone makes us mad or if a loved one is done wrong is the same fight we have to have about our vision. You should expect enemies along the way. Enemies to vision include distractions, discouragement and opposition. Your enemies will be outside factors that will attempt to hinder you but cannot stop you.

The only enemy that can ultimately stop you and the one that really matters is the person in the mirror! Oftentimes, we are our biggest enemy. Thinking that we're not good enough, smart enough or strong enough to handle it. We must work continually to overcome ourselves.

Personal Challenge for Lesson #8

Questions to Ask Yourself: What is the vision for your life? What are you passionate about? What are your unique skills and talents that align with that? Who are the people that you would need to support or be a part it?

Assignment: Think about the impact you want to have in this world. It could be in the business arena or the community. Consider the issues that concern you and the audience(s) that you desire to reach. Contemplating all these things and how they work together will help you to discover your vision. Put it someplace where you can reference it often whether it's on a board, a sheet of paper or your phone. Then, make a list of all your skills and talents that you can use to help you accomplish your vision. Make a list of the people that you will need to be a part of your support system as well. After all of the above is done, commit to three short-term goals that will get you moving forward towards your vision. Some examples of short-term goals could include taking up a course to increase your skills and understanding, joining a professional association to build relationships with like-minded people or doing some research to learn more about your target audience.

Bottom Line: You cannot be a leader without vision. Discover it, write it down, review it often and make sure you see it correctly. Go after it with all your heart because it's worth fighting for.

Coming From the Heart of a Leader

Lesson #9

Build Relationships

One day, I was getting lunch with a dear friend of mine. We work together in many facets of my life including business and community work. Since she's seen many sides of me and I value her opinion, I asked her what one my strengths were and surprisingly she said to me that I was good at developing intimate relationships. I never really thought about it that way until she mentioned it because that's just me. I love to develop meaningful relationships with people so I'm not quick to connect with everyone. I need to know who's among me and what I'm working with so I'll know how to proceed. I like the term relationship building rather than networking. When you are building a relationship with a person, especially for business purposes, you are connecting with them and learning how you can help one another. You create reciprocity and people are more likely to treat you right. When you are focused on networking, you put on a fake face and you're solely focused on connecting with people to see what you can get out of them that will help you move ahead. That's how you can end up working with people that don't mean you well instead of being selective. You have to decide whether someone is a great fit for you and you for them. I'd rather have quality relationships with those that I'm in business with than to just have another connection. It's the same when building a relationship with those who you are leading.

There are few components of relationship building that will aid anyone who desires to improve in this area in any type of relationship.

- **Genuine care.** Have a genuine interest in getting to know people so that you can know how to serve them well. One of my previous managers used to tell me "people don't care how much you know until they know how much you care". Let people see your heart, if it is indeed genuine. If your heart is not genuine then that is a personal issue that needs to be resolved. If people think that you only want to talk to them for personal gain, then they could really care less about what you have to say. We can't be so focused on what we have to say that we miss what others have to say. People like to be known and understood. As you are getting to know others, look for the best in them. While you are in conversation with them, be an active listener and be observant. Listen for clues on how you can relate to them and how you can add value to them. Take note of their interests, likes, dislikes, motivations, frustrations, etc. You'll be surprised at what people will share with you if you have a listening ear. In the end it will help you but you have to put forth that effort, especially, if it's someone that you desire to work with in any capacity. The level of investment in the relationship may also depend on the type of relationship you want to have with the person.

- **Doing right by others.** Treat others the way that you would want to be treated. Now, does that mean that you should treat people according to what would make you happy? Not necessarily. It's about showing honor and appreciation for others because that's what you would want. It's about respecting and valuing others because that's what you would want. It's about being honest and truthful with others because that's what you would want. Sometimes we get it a little twisted and we can treat other people based on our own preferences rather than treating them based on their unique needs. For instance, I've been guilty of giving gifts to friends and loved ones based on what I would expect to receive rather than what would connect to and be meaningful to them. During those times, I knew very well that I was really thinking about myself when I got the gifts.

- **Trust.** Trust is not given but it is earned. People have to trust you and you have to be willing to trust them. Trust is only built through relationship and being consistent in that relationship. When you see that someone is reliable and consistent whether it's convenient or not, you are more likely to deem them as trustworthy. Sometimes, you can tell if a person is trustworthy not only by how they treat you but also by observing how they treat other people around you. I make it a point to do this when I'm just getting to know people. I've experienced situations at work where people will come to me and gossip about a colleague or put them down but never address the person directly. I'll have to encourage that they deal with the person so I won't be caught up in it and it's a red flag to me to be mindful how much trust I really want to give this person. I've also experienced the opposite where I've seen the same person always covering their team members and looking for the best in them. At that point, I know that's someone that I can trust because their intentions are good and they're consistent.

- **Approachability.** No one will want to talk to you if you come off as someone who is distant or easily offended. Sometimes, we stay on the defense and take everything personal. We have to be willing to let our guard down a little. Take precaution but you still have to do it to some extent. I remember worrying about proving myself as a leader and trying to keep myself at a distance from everyone else because I wanted to gain their respect and I felt that they would no longer respect me if they got too close to me. I felt like I had to be perfect and couldn't make any mistakes because then that would mess up my "image" but it's not about being perfect. Even if mistakes are made, all we have to do is own up to them, learn from them and move on. There is a balance. You don't have to tell everyone all your deep dark secrets as if you're best buds. Just be friendly and have a welcoming demeanor. I have to constantly work on myself in this area because I am an introvert. I like to spend a lot of time to myself and I don't like to talk to people all the time. Don't get me wrong, I love people but the amount of time I spend in group settings can only be in small dosages. With this in mind, I have to be mindful to speak to others when I'm in their presence so I won't come across as antisocial and distant.

- **Availability.** You can't be so busy that you don't have room to spend time with people. We have to be around, especially, in case of emergencies or needed assistance. In my role as a clinical systems coordinator, I was responsible for mentoring the data team and being available for any questions or issue escalations. There were times when I was very busy working on other duties and they would reach out to me with questions that they had and I would be a little bothered because I was so focused on getting other important tasks done. However, I had to realize that it didn't matter what I had going on, my job as their leader was to be available to them. I couldn't appear to them as being bothered because then that would discourage them to come to me in the future. If there were times when I wasn't available right away, I still acknowledged their request and reassured them that I would follow up by a certain time.

- **Communication.** There are no good relationships without effective communication. We have to learn to be better communicators. It doesn't matter how great of a vision you may have or how great of an idea that you may have, if you are not able to take your thoughts and clearly communicate them to others then you will not be able to connect with them. Even as a leader, if people don't understand what you are saying then it will be hard for them to follow you. Sometimes, this can be a struggle when you have one thing in mind, you know where you're going and you tell others about it but somehow they either did not hear what you had to say or took it a completely different way. It leaves you feeling like how in the world did they take it that way because it's not even what you thought you said. We have to remember that though we know exactly what we mean, other people don't so it will take more effort to communicate it and find a way to speak their language. Sometimes, the same message can be taken a completely different way depending on the person, their perception and experiences.

- **Letting the relationship develop naturally.** Don't try to force or make a relationship work. Sometimes we have to relax and let it develop over time. No good relationship is developed overnight. Just be your authentic self and do your part to add value to others. We also have to realize that we're not a great fit for everyone and that's okay. There will be people who we don't desire to a build relationship with and there will be people who don't desire to build a relationship with us. This may be due to different interests, goals, values, perspectives, etc. Not to say that we should be mean or rude to anyone but understand that it's a part of life and shouldn't be taken personally. For instance, one of my good friends is very into politics and I'm not so if we're at an event together and she comes across someone who's in politics she's going to be engaging in conversation with them and will connect with them on a level that I cannot. However, I can't get mad or think that the person doesn't like me if they desire to develop a relationship with her and not me because we have completely different interests.

Personal Challenge for Lesson #9

Questions to Ask Yourself: How would you rate yourself when it comes developing a relationship with other people? How you rate your current relationships? What are you good at and what are you not so good at?

Assignment: On a scale of one to ten, with ten being the highest and one being the lowest, rate yourself based on where you feel you are when it comes to your ability to build relationships with others. Considering the information that was discussed in this lesson, make a note as to why you gave yourself the rating that you did. Then, get someone else's feedback to see how they would rate you and why. After this exercise is done, identify two areas that you're good at that will aid you in developing relationships and two more areas that may be a hindrance for you. For instance, one good area could be that you have a genuine concern for the needs of others and a hindrance could be that you have a habit of trying to force people to like you.

Bottom Line: Relationship building is essential and more important than networking and just having another connection. People don't want to work with or follow anyone that they don't have a relationship with.

Lesson #10

There's a Time to Lead and a Time to Follow

When I first started working as a coordinator for a pharmaceutical company, I was so excited and ready to embark on any opportunity to show my leadership abilities. During this time, they started a Toastmasters Club. The purpose of Toastmasters is to sharpen your communication and leadership skills. When the club was first introduced to the company, they asked if anyone would be interested in taking on different roles such as President, Vice President, Treasury, Time Keeper, Official, etc. Immediately, because I know that I am a leader, I thought that I should probably run for the President or the Vice President position because I knew that I would be good at it since I am gifted in the area of leadership. However, I got the feeling that a leadership role in this club was not the best place for me at that time. At this point, I had just started working for the company and I hadn't even hit the two-week mark or started to develop a good rapport with my colleagues. How could I expect to be successful in this role when I was still trying to learn my new job and I didn't know the people around me well enough that I could be someone that they would vote for and want to follow. I had to learn that not every opportunity is for me to lead or take on but sometimes I have to be willing to follow someone else's lead. This can be very difficult for leaders to do, especially, if you are used to being in charge all of the time. Great leaders are great followers. They know how to balance when to lead and when to follow. They are able to adjust themselves in both situations because it's all about being a part of the team. There's more than one person who can lead and there's more than one person who has something great to offer. There has to be a shared responsibility.

In order to follow, we have to be willing to be team players. Here are some tools to keep in mind in order to operate as a part of a team.

- **Have the mindset of a team player.** When you have the mindset of a team player you are focused on collaboration and you see every role on the team as significant. You see others as contributors rather than competition. Two great ideas are always better than one. We have to be open to hearing someone else's perspective and letting them share their strengths. It doesn't matter what role you play on the team because every role is needed. Even if you are not the designated leader, your role is still important.
- **Play well with others.** Be nice. It can be difficult at times but it's not that hard. Don't try to push others to the side so that the spotlight can be on you. When individuals on your team are succeeding congratulate

them. When other individuals on your team are struggling, find out what you can do to help them if possible. I'll admit that I've never liked working with people. I'm most comfortable with solo projects but I can't be that way all the time.

- **Don't leave others behind.** When you are working on a project with a group of people, don't be so focused on you understanding the vision and owning your part that you don't care or even notice if others are left behind who may be struggling to catch up. Everybody has to move forward together.

- **Cover your teammates.** When people tell you something in secret, don't be so quick to share it. When people make mistakes, don't be so quick to throw them under the bus when in the company of others. Deal with issues in house but there should be a unified front.

- **Delegate when necessary.** You will drive yourself crazy trying to do everyone's part. It's okay to delegate tasks that we may not be particularly good at but someone else is. No one is skilled at everything. We also may need to delegate due to time constraints. Sometimes, you simply just don't have the time to do it on your own and you need some assistance.

Now that we've addressed that there will be times when it's most beneficial to follow, let's discuss those times when it doesn't pay to follow and someone has to step up to take the lead. When you are a leader, you shouldn't simply do things or not do things because of what everyone else is doing. There will be times when people aren't doing anything different because everyone's doing the same things and no one's taking the lead. For instance, some weeks ago I decided to go to Walmart to pick up a few personal items. When I finished all of my shopping for that time, I proceeded to go to the self-checkout section. When I arrived, there was a line of people ahead of me and there were about six stations open. As I continued to wait in line, I noticed that there was one particular station that everyone kept passing but would never use it. I asked one of the young ladies in front of me, if there was something wrong with it as to why people weren't using it. Her only response to me was I'm not sure but I think it may be broken because no one else is using it. It seemed fine to me and I didn't see a sign to indicate that it was out of order so her response wasn't enough for me. I made my way to the station and sure enough it worked just fine and the same young lady that had been in front of me waiting for another station ended up using it after I was done. I could imagine how she felt waiting in the line all that time simply because of what other people were doing. From this story, I learned three simple yet important lessons about taking the lead.

- **Have a mind of your own.** Don't think that everyone else is always right and you are always wrong. Just because it's popular doesn't mean that it's the right way to go. Do some investigation, ask questions, form your own thoughts and opinions. One of my mentors, told me once before that you have to be confident in what you know until people can prove to you and give you good reason to see it another way. It's not about being rebellious and challenging things for the sake of being different but owning the privilege of thinking for yourself.

- **Don't miss out on great opportunities because of others.** We can miss out on great opportunities at work and in life in general if we are always going with the crowd. It doesn't matter who's not doing what and who's tried to do it and failed. That doesn't have to be your story. It doesn't matter if everyone has adopted a particular belief. It doesn't have to be yours. Just because nobody likes that coworker and can't get along with him or her doesn't mean that you have to adopt the same attitude without even trying to get to know the person for yourself.

- **Some people won't have the courage to change until you change.** Thinking back to the young lady who was in the line at Walmart with me, she wouldn't have tried the pay station that everyone kept passing had she not seen it work for me. Believe it or not, there are some people who are looking at you as an encouragement whether or not they tell you. They are waiting for you to get moving so that they can see what can be made possible for them. Don't underestimate the importance of your life. Don't wait for someone else to be the example, you set the example!

Personal Challenge for Lesson #10

Questions to Ask Yourself: Are you able to adjust when you need to follow or when you need to lead? What are some ways that you can be better in both areas? Would others be encouraged by the life you are leading?

Assignment: Think about one or two examples of when you struggled to be a follower and identify how you could have done better. For instance, it could be that during groups meetings you always have something to say but you never stop to think that maybe someone else wants to contribute to the conversation. Now, think about one or two examples of when you struggled to take the lead and identify how you could have done better in this area as well. For instance, it could be that you allow the fear of rejection hinder you from expressing your thoughts to others when you feel you have a great idea about something.

Bottom Line: Both followers and leaders are needed to get the job done. It is very well possible and necessary for a leader to operate in both areas.

Lesson #11

Learn to Work with Other Leaders

The topic of how leaders can work with other leaders really hit home with me and got me thinking after a conversation that I had with my Mary Kay consultant who happens to be a leadership consultant as well. We met at Barnes and Nobles so that I could get my new products and to just connect and catch up on life. I was telling her about how my business endeavors were going and a part of which included my writing endeavors. At some point, we got into a conversation about the struggles when it comes to leaders who are from the millennial generation working with leaders who are from the baby boomers generation. It made me think about my own personal struggles when dealing with leaders who are more experienced than I am as well leaders who didn't have as much experience as I did leading in certain areas. When I pondered on our conversation, I took away three valuable lessons that are to be considered when leaders are working with each other.

- **Leaders contribute to their leaders too.** When it comes to the mentor and mentee relationship, there's this misconception that the mentee should always learn from their mentor but the mentor can never learn from them. If the mentor does learn from them then it's seen as a slight against them as if they're inadequate or missed something that they should have learned beforehand but many times this way of thinking is inaccurate. If it is not understood in the beginning that each person can and should add value to the mentor and mentee relationship then there may tend to be a power struggle between the two. There has to be a mutual benefit for any relationship to be healthy. Leaders don't just take and take from those who are leading them but they look for ways that they can help them as well. That doesn't necessarily mean that the mentee will teach their leader something in the area that they are leading though that could very well be the case because no one knows everything. The way that the mentee could add value to their leader may also be shown by them providing the leader with a new perspective on things, asking difficult questions, giving them encouragement or even giving the leader feedback on areas where they feel improvement is needed. For instance, in my role as a coordinator over a data team, I had a mentor who would coach me and provide me with feedback on areas of improvement in how I could lead the team more effectively. It took me some time to really get used to the role and it was a little intimidating at first to share my ideas with her because I felt like what she had to say would have been a better idea or that she wouldn't have wanted to hear it because she was already very knowledgeable. However, I began to struggle less when I realized that she not only wanted to help me do my job better but she was also open to hearing my thoughts on how different processes could be better. That's not to say that we always agreed on everything but she welcomed the open conversation and I could tell that she had good intentions. She was also open to getting feedback from me on how effective she was as a mentor and that is how it should be.

- **How to deal when you are a new leader working with experienced leaders.** When you are a new leader working with experienced leaders, you should definitely be confident in who you are and in your abilities but you also have to be careful to temper your attitude because you don't want to come across as arrogant or overly confident. If you're not mindful to temper how you portray your confidence, then you could be seen as a threat or as a know it all who's just trying to be the next big thing. For instance, if someone were to tell you that you have really great ideas, you don't have to say things like I know I do or I'm glad somebody finally noticed! That may certainly come across as cocky and will be a turn off. You could simply thank them for bringing it to your attention and how you strive to be a valuable asset wherever you go. It will come across much better than the first response. Don't think you know it all. You have to be teachable. Take the time to honor them for the work that they have done and acknowledge them for how they have helped you in some way. Show them the same respect and appreciation that you would want to receive. Give them honest feedback when requested. Build a relationship with them in such a way that they learn to see you as someone who is trustworthy. At the same time, don't belittle yourself or think that you have to hide the great qualities that you have so that they won't feel uncomfortable. If you come across experienced leaders who look down on you or don't have a teachable attitude, don't internalize it but realize that's a personal issue that they have to deal with. You also have to learn to be assertive when necessary so that others will take you seriously.

- **How to deal when you are an experienced leader working with new leaders.** When you are an experienced leader working with new leaders, don't lose confidence in who you are and in the work that you have done over the years. If you lose your confidence, you'll give into the temptation to be concerned about pulling rank when they start to grow and you'll try to prove to them that you're not on the same level. Treat them based on how you would want a leader to treat you even if you haven't had positive experiences yourself. Coach them and give them tips on how they can be more effective or what they need to be mindful of. Teach them to avoid certain roadblocks that you've seen or experienced rather than expecting them to have to go through the exact same struggles that you did. Their story should be better than your story because they have wisdom and foreknowledge from you. Don't expect them to have the same journey and experiences as you did in order to get to where you are. Yes, there are certain things that we all need to go learn such working hard, making sacrifices, and going above the call of duty but we have to be careful about thinking that our path should be the standard for everyone else. Don't give into the temptation that you cannot help them or that they will not listen to you because they may know a lot or even know things that you do not know. Be open to what you could potentially learn from them as a person or from the relationship that you have with them. Teach them from a place of genuine concern for their success. Realize that when they are moving forward under your tutelage that means that you are doing your job right. One of my previous managers once told me that "your success is my success" and that is a very true statement. If I was moving forward in my career, it was a compliment to my manager because she was the one leading me so it was not a point of intimidation. Let your experience with them cause you to grow and challenge yourself.

Personal Challenge for Lesson #11

Questions to Ask Yourself: When you think about your leadership experiences, in which of the three lessons did you find yourself struggling? What are some reasons why you struggled? What could you have done better?

Assignment: Think about how well you work with the leaders that are in your life whether they are more experienced or less experienced than you are. Concerning the leader(s) that you follow, commit to one action item that you can do that will add value to them. For instance, an action item could be that you send them an encouraging note to let them know that you appreciate them for being a great role model. Concerning the leader(s) that follow you, commit to one action item that you can do that will show your appreciation and encourage them to know that they are valuable to you. For instance, an action item could be that you reassure them that you benefit from the skills and ideas that they bring to the table and just others.

Bottom Line: A leader to leader relationship should be mutually beneficial. It doesn't matter how much experience you do or do not have, everyone has something to learn and everyone has something to teach.

Lesson #12

Deal with Issues

My very first job out of college was in data management
working for a biotechnology company. While I worked there
one of my job responsibilities included leading our department
meetings. I would gather and organize the agenda topics for the
meetings when it was my turn to facilitate. I had been working
there for a few months and during this time there were issues
between our department and the risk management department
with people not communicating with one another,
understanding the values that each of the roles in each
department brings and what the other department wasn't
doing in an effective manner. Due to this, there had been a bit
of tension with the other department and people would often
express their concerns and frustrations. The way that our
department meetings were set up is that they were very open
for honest dialog and our motto was "what's goes on in this
room stays in this room" so that the team wouldn't be afraid to
express what was really on their minds. It started to concern me
that we continued to discuss the issues that were going on with
other departments while we failed to address the issues within
our team and how we could make them better so I wanted to
express my concerns in our next department meeting that I
would happen to facilitate that time. I'll admit that I hadn't

always been a person who was willing to handle conflict but I had such a passion and strong conviction about what I believed to be right that it superseded my fears of what others would think so I couldn't keep silent. Although, I knew that it wasn't the happiest topic to address because sometimes it's difficult to put aside what others are doing wrong and examine ourselves to see what we are doing wrong. Always looking at others keeps us from accepting the responsibility of our own actions and seeing what we can do to make the situation better. Keeping all of this in mind, I cleared it with my manager to get his thoughts and he felt the same way that I did in that it would a great topic to discuss.

When it came time for the meeting, I expressed my concerns and talked about how the first step in us making the relationship better with the other departments starts when we make things better within our own team and show them how a team is supposed to operate. I specifically asked them if they wanted examples of how we hadn't been the best team players with one another so they could understand where I was coming from and they agreed that they wanted to hear specifics. I proceeded to share examples of what I had seen in our group with gossiping and showing partiality which was definitely not conducive to a teamwork environment. I encouraged team to discuss the issue so that it would be squashed before we left the meeting. No one had anything to say but I could tell that people were mad. After the meeting was over, I had some people who commended me for being willing to address a topic that most would avoid and of course I had others who were so mad at me that they didn't even want to talk to me. It wasn't my intention to offend anyone but I had to share the truth because I cared. Since it concerned me that individuals no longer wanted to talk to me, I reached out to them to talk to them individually so that we could reconcile our differences. There were some relationships that were mended and we were able to move on, however, there were others that still didn't want to have anything to do with me. It really bothered me but there was nothing more that I could do. I knew that I couldn't apologize for what I said and that over time it would make our team better though it stung for a moment.

As I think about this experience in my life I am reminded of two valuable lessons when it comes to dealing with issues.

- **Not dealing with issues causes division.** When you are not willing to address issues, they become infectious to the entire team and grow into a bigger mess. You should always promote peace and unity. Avoiding issues and acting like they don't exist is not the way to do this but it is done through addressing the issues head on. Confrontation and conflict is uncomfortable for anyone involved but it cannot be avoided. I've been in work environments where there were cliques, bullying and negativity but no one, including management, wanted to address it. I've also been in work environments where it was the complete opposite so when team members went to management talking negatively about a coworker they would automatically be encouraged to bring the other person in so that they could all talk face to face and both sides of the stories could be heard. That way the issue was settled fairly quickly rather than being entertained. It's one thing to have someone that you can talk to so that you can vent but if not careful it can easily turn into a gossip session. Now, not every issue requires that you address it with the next person. You have to pick and choose your battles. Sometimes, it's just not worth the possible consequences of saying something. However, it still needs to be addressed whether you address within yourself or with someone else. Oftentimes, we use the idea of dealing with issues on our own as a cop out. We're most comfortable with just dealing with issues within ourselves and we say that we're over it but we're really not and it shows in our actions. When it gets to the point that the issues we are experiencing influences our work ethic as well as others and it hinders a team effort then handling it within yourself is simply not enough. It requires that we get "touch skin" as they say and develop emotional and mental fortitude so that we can face those difficult situations.

- **Be able to give and receive constructive criticism.** Don't dish out what you what you are not willing to take. Most times, it can be easy for us to tell people what's on our minds but when it comes to people doing the same to us, we end up end falling apart and being all over the place. As a leader it is not your job to tell people what they want to hear. It is your job to lead them and tell them the truth with care even if it's not what they want to hear in that moment. People don't need someone who will be overly impressed by them because that person will always give you praises and never challenge you. People also don't need someone who will be intimidated by them because that person will always give them negative criticism or never offer any words of encouragement. Oftentimes, we fear giving constructive criticism because we don't want to deal with the possible effects of making a person mad. However, people will actually respect you more when you are upfront and honest with them even if they don't tell you. One of the reasons why giving and receiving constructive feedback from others can be difficult is because we don't always know how to give it or receive it due to the lack of having seen it before. Usually, people do what they know and what's been done to them. We have to learn that there is a way to say things. This is a continual learning process even for me. We have to tell the truth with care and without attacking the person but addressing the action, the situation and how it came across. People automatically shut down when you start using terms that attack their character. Whenever you tell someone what they did wrong or what they need to improve on, help them to come to a solution on how to get it right so that they can move forward. Don't just point out their faults because there's no growth in that. Always be humble and understanding of where the person is and how you would want to be treated because you never know when you'll make a mistake and need the same understanding. It is also very critical when dealing in this area that you have an established relationship with the person or they will not want to hear you out. One of my mentors has often said that correction outside of relationship is nothing more than offense and I couldn't agree more.

Personal Challenge for Lesson #12

Questions to Ask Yourself: How have you handled issues in the past? Did you face them or did you try to avoid them? How have your current strategies been working for you? In what areas can you improve? What steps can you begin to take to implement the improvement?

Assignment: Think back on one issue you've experienced recently and how you dealt with it. If you are not proud of how you handled it then make a note of what you could do differently the next time you are presented with the same situation. It could be that you have a colleague who is always disrespectful to you without any cause and you always keep silent about it. An area for improvement could be to find a way to address the person to see if the two of you can make amends before you attempt to address it with management. Moving forward, when you encounter an issue with an individual or a group of people, challenge yourself to face it rather than avoiding it. Get into the habit for dealing with it head on.

Bottom Line: Leaders don't run from issues but they deal with them head on. Examine how well you respond in this area and how you can better position yourself for those difficult times.

Coming From the Heart of a Leader

Lesson #13

Your Influence Should Be Evident

During the time that I worked for a clinical research organization in the area of project management, I had the privilege of meeting with one of the VPs that was over our division. She was always open to meeting with me if I ever wanted to talk. I looked up to her so whenever there was time, I would talk to her to get her advice and wisdom on leadership. At one particular meeting that we had, I discussed with her my desire for a career change and how I was passionate about leadership. I remember trying to express to her and somehow prove myself as a leader but the feedback she gave challenged me to examine myself yet it was great wisdom. She informed me that based on her observations she couldn't tell that I was a leader because I didn't have any visible actions that she could see in regards to my interactions with others. As I've mentioned in previous lessons, I am most comfortable staying to myself so she wouldn't see me talking to a lot of people. The perception that I gave off was that I was a little distant from my team. She goes on to express that results are what people want to see and it's not so much about working harder than everyone else but producing better results. After that conversation, I really had to look inwardly to see whether my actions lined up with who I said I was. The truth of the matter is I shouldn't have to go on ranting around talking about how great I am because the way that I live and my impact on others should speak for me. There were indeed people around me that could attest to how I've impacted them but I couldn't get settled there. The fact that she had some doubts let me know that I needed to make some improvements. I am determined now more than ever that the world will know my name every day that I wake up because I don't let life just happen to me but I create the day that I want to have by being intentional to influence someone else for the better.

The following lessons will help anyone to live everyday with the intention to lead with impact.

- **Make others greater.** When you decide that you want to be leader, you have made a decision that you will serve others and make them greater than yourself. Now, this does not mean that others are better than you in the sense that you are making yourself inferior to them because that would not be conducive to a healthy relationship. Most times, we're happy to teach others as long as they are in a sense behind us but the moment that they start to seemingly get ahead of us and start teaching us new things then the inferiority issue kicks in. In actuality, it should be encouragement for you to see the results of your investment in them. As I think about the great leaders in my life, I am privileged to have them as examples of what this looks like. They push me forward, they teach me the valuable lessons that they've learned and the mistakes they've made so I won't have to go through the same things. They don't get mad when I succeed but they celebrate me. They present me with opportunities to exercise my leadership skills and they allow me to be me. The greatest gift that you can give someone is acceptance of who they are while pushing them to be the best that they can be. They continuously show me what it means to sacrifice for the good of others and for that I am thankful. Now, there are two ways that you can make others greater. The first way is by teaching them things that you have learned. Find out where their knowledge is lacking and position yourself in such a way that you can be an advisor to them. The second way is by pulling out the potential in others. In order to pull out the potential in others, you have to be willing to look for and recognize what their potential is. Find out what they're good at and what their strengths are. Encourage them in their strong areas and help them to identify opportunities where they can exercise it.

- **Influence culture.** The culture is kind of like the way of life or the feel of the environment at a particular company or an organization. I've worked in environments where everyone was stressed and only concerned about their own work. I've also worked in environments where the people were laid back, lively and supportive of one another. As a leader, it should be your goal to influence the culture wherever you are. You can even influence culture without being publically recognized for it. For instance, during the time that I worked in project management, we had gotten a new director and she had to come to our location to visit. There were a lot of changes and challenges in the group that she had to familiarize herself with and we were experiencing the growing pains in an attempt to make our department better. During her visit, we were encouraged to give her feedback on how we thought things were going and present to her any ideas that we had. After her visit ended, the group came together to discuss any pending concerns and how productive we felt her visit was. Many people expressed their concerns and how they didn't understand why certain decisions were being made. They were legitimate concerns that had already been discussed before but it started to become a little negative. Since I felt that the conversation was heading in the wrong direction, I expressed to the group that my only feedback or concern was that I didn't get to tell our director thank you for taking the time to come visit us to develop a good rapport, discuss the future direction of the department and to hear our thoughts on things. I also expressed that though we all know she's made some mistakes and was still learning our group, we should be a little more understanding because we all make mistakes and we don't know all the pressure that she may be experiencing because we're not in her position. I felt like everyone heard what I said because I presented it in a way to say that said I could do something better myself rather than just pointing the finger at everyone else. However, I didn't know how impactful it was until another director in our division came to visit. When he came to visit, I was informed how after his presentation was over, everyone in my group went up to him just to say thank you for coming though it wasn't a public announcement that I encouraged this new behavior in our group.

Personal Challenge for Lesson #13

Questions to Ask Yourself: Do you intentionally influence others? How is your impact evident? How would you describe the culture of your company or organization? What can you do to make it better?

Assignment: Consider your company or organization. Think about one way that you can begin to influence those around you. For instance, you could identify the strengths of those around you and remind them that what they have to offer is beneficial to the group. Now, think about one way that you can influence the culture around you. For instance, if most of your colleagues tend to be negative you could encourage them to know that they control whether they'll have a good or bad day no matter what their circumstances are.

Bottom Line: Not only do leaders influence individuals but they also influence the culture they're placed in. Influence is power. Use it wisely.

Conclusion

Now that I have shared with you the thirteen lessons that I've learned about leadership, it is my sincere desire that you have been both challenged and inspired to become a greater leader than you are today. First, it starts with you and the internal work that needs to be done through self-examination. Then, you will be able to have the impact that you desire to see in the lives of others. At the beginning of book, I mentioned that each of the lessons fall under one of three categories which include what leadership really is, the principles to be applied before you lead and the principles to be applied when you lead. You'll notice that seven of the thirteen lessons fall under the second category because your leadership ability has a lot to do with you and less to do with other people. You are the most important factor in the equation. Not in a selfish way but in a selfless way in that when you become better it will in turn position you to offer something of substance to others that will make them better. I encourage you to implement the principles and strategies that were shared. Make it a thirteen-day challenge where each day you focus on completing the assignment in one of the lessons until you get through all of them.

Author Bio and Contact Information

Portia Daniels, the CEO of Unrestricted Excellence, is a leadership speaker and advisor who is passionate about teaching leaders how to operate in wisdom and in excellence. She is best described as regal, insightful, poised, and joyful. She is a graduate of East Carolina University with a Bachelor of Arts in Psychology. She has over 5 years of leadership experience in the clinical research and pharmaceutical industries in various areas to include project management, training, mentoring, facilitating and public speaking. Currently, Portia resides in Raleigh, North Carolina.

For more information about Portia Daniels, visit

https://about.me/portiadaniels

https://www.facebook.com/unrestrictedexcellence

https://www.linkedin.com/in/portiadaniels

www.ingramcontent.com/pod-product-compliance
Lightning Source LLC
Chambersburg PA
CBHW061145180526
45170CB00002B/630